With Wings Like Eagles

Creative Writing For Christian Teens

Old Testament

Cheryl Pryor

Arlington & Amelia

Copyright © 2018 Cheryl Pryor

Arlington & Amelia Publishing

ArlingtonAmeliaPub@cfl.rr.com

ISBN:1-886541-39-6
ISBN:13-978-1-886541-39-9

TABLE OF CONTENTS

HOW TO USE THIS BOOK

'With Wings Like Eagles' is an introduction to creative writing for Christian teens focusing on scriptures and living a Godly lifestyle.

'With Wings Like Eagles' is meant to encourage, uplift, and inspire teens to fill their lives with love, joy, faith, and good works.

This book can be used as a teen Bible study, part of a homeschool requirement for a high school ½ credit, or for the purpose of edifying your teen and encouraging them to grow spiritually.

'With Wings Like Eagles' is part 1 of a 2 part series. This book, the first book in the series, focuses on the Old Testament. This book can be used on it's own or together with 'A Humble Spirit' part 2 in the series which focuses on the New Testament.

If you are homeschooling, you may wish to use this course for a high school ½ credit towards an English/Creative Writing credit or for Bible. If you are planning on using this book for a high school credit, check with your state or local homeschooling group to see how this can be used for your child's curriculum.

The book can be used in the order it is written, completing one chapter before going on to the next or each day use an assignment from a different chapter. It is entirely up to you.

Other Books by Cheryl Pryor

A Humble Spirit: New Testament Creative Writing For Christian Teens

With Wings Like Eagles: Old Testament Creative Writing For Christian Teens

The Big Book of Old Testament Bible Trivia

The Big Book of New Testament Bible Trivia

Living The Word of God

Women In History Trivia

Where In The U.S. Am I?

Where In The World Am I?

The Big Book of Presidential Trivia

The Big Book of First Ladies Trivia

Presidents, First Ladies, & First Family Trivia

Presidents Trivia Challenge

First Family Trivia

Children Of The Presidents

American Revolution & The Birth of A Nation Trivia

Chosen

Pregnancy Journal

Precious Moments

Treasured Moments of My Child

My Mother's Life Story

My Father's Life Story

How Much Do You *Really* Know About The Love Of Your Life?

Couples Game Night Challenge

RV Travel & Expense Journal

Wedding Survival Guide

Write Now

Legacy

Children's Books

My Child's Keepsake Journal

Trivia For Kids: The Presidents

Trivia For Kids: First Ladies

From the series: The Sullivan Family Series

Savannah In The Big Move

Savannah On Stage

Savannah On Horseback

Savannah in Look What Followed Me Home

Savannah & The Grumpy Neighbor

Savannah & The Mad Scientist

From the series: Savannah's World Travels Series

Savannah's Disney World Celebration

Savannah Goes To Paris

1

Scriptures As Writing Starting Points

In this section a verse from Psalms or Proverbs will be given.

Write how the scripture applies to your life and what it means to you

1) Psalm 37:5 – Commit your way to the Lord.

_____

_____

_____

_____

_____

_____

_____

_____

2.) Psalm 39:1 – I will guard my ways that I may not sin with my tongue; I will guard my mouth as with a muzzle.

_____

_____

_____

_____

_____

_____

_____

_____

_____

_____

_____

_____

_____

_____

3.) Proverbs 1:10 – If sinners entice you, do not consent.

_____

_____

_____

_____

_____

_____

_____

_____

_____

_____

_____

_____

_____

_____

4.) Proverbs 5:21 – For the ways of a man are before the eyes of the Lord and He watches all his paths.

_____

_____

_____

_____

_____

_____

_____

_____

_____

_____

_____

_____

_____

_____

5.) Proverbs 10:2 – Ill-gotten gains do not profit.

_____

_____

_____

_____

_____

_____

_____

_____

_____

_____

_____

_____

_____

_____

_____

6.) Proverbs 11:2 – When pride comes, then comes dishonor, but with the humble is wisdom.

_____

_____

_____

_____

_____

_____

_____

_____

_____

_____

_____

_____

_____

7.) Proverbs 11:13 – He who goes about as a tale-bearer reveals secrets, but he who is trustworthy conceals a matter.

_____

_____

_____

_____

_____

_____

_____

_____

_____

_____

_____

_____

_____

8.) Proverbs 12:14 – The deeds of a man's hands will return to him.

_____

_____

_____

_____

_____

_____

_____

_____

_____

_____

_____

_____

_____

_____

_____

9.) Proverbs 12:20 – Deceit is in the heart of those who devise evil.

_____

_____

_____

_____

_____

_____

_____

_____

_____

_____

_____

_____

_____

_____

_____

_____

10.) Proverbs 13:20 – He who walks with wise men will be wise; but the companion of fools will suffer harm.

_____

_____

_____

_____

_____

_____

_____

_____

_____

_____

_____

_____

_____

_____

_____

_____

2

Daily Bible Reading

Make a habit of reading your Bible daily.

You may choose to read a verse you may have highlighted in your Bible that has special meaning to you to apply towards your life or begin reading one of the books of the Bible.

Whichever you choose, each day write the verse or book, chapter, and verses you read and write any comments or thoughts you have about what you read.

Keep track of your reading and thoughts on what you read for the next ten days.

Date: _____

I read: _____

My thoughts: _____

_____

_____

_____

_____

_____

_____

_____

_____

_____

_____

_____

_____

_____

_____

_____

_____

_____

Date: _____

I read: _____

My thoughts: _____

_____

_____

_____

_____

_____

_____

_____

_____

_____

_____

_____

_____

_____

_____

_____

_____

_____

Date: _____

I read: _____

My thoughts: _____

_____

_____

_____

_____

_____

_____

_____

_____

_____

_____

_____

_____

_____

_____

_____

_____

_____

Date: _____

I read: _____

My thoughts: _____

_____

_____

_____

_____

_____

_____

_____

_____

_____

_____

_____

_____

_____

_____

_____

_____

Date: _____

I read: _____

My thoughts: _____

_____

_____

_____

_____

_____

_____

_____

_____

_____

_____

_____

_____

_____

_____

_____

_____

_____

Date: _____

I read: _____

My thoughts: _____

_____

_____

_____

_____

_____

_____

_____

_____

_____

_____

_____

_____

_____

_____

_____

_____

Date: _____

I read: _____

My thoughts: _____

_____

_____

_____

_____

_____

_____

_____

_____

_____

_____

_____

_____

_____

_____

_____

_____

_____

Date: _____

I read: _____

My thoughts: _____

_____

_____

_____

_____

_____

_____

_____

_____

_____

_____

_____

_____

_____

_____

_____

Date: _____

I read: _____

My thoughts: _____

_____

_____

_____

_____

_____

_____

_____

_____

_____

_____

_____

_____

_____

_____

_____

Date: _____

I read: _____

My thoughts: _____

_____

_____

_____

_____

_____

_____

_____

_____

_____

_____

_____

_____

_____

_____

_____

3

Vocabulary Words

Write the definition of each word below. If you are unsure of the definition, use the concordance in your Bible.

1) faith

_____

_____

_____

2) pray; pray without ceasing

_____

_____

_____

3) angel

_____

_____

_____

4) edification

_____

_____

_____

5) merciful

_____

_____

_____

6) grace

_____

_____

_____

7) ministry

_____

_____

_____

8) obey

_____

_____

9) creation

_____

_____

_____

10) encourage

_____

_____

_____

Write how each of the vocabulary words applies to your own life.

1. _____

_____

_____

_____

2. _____

_____

_____

3. _____

_____

_____

_____

4. _____

_____

_____

_____

5. _____

_____

_____

_____

6. _____

_____

_____

_____

7. _____

_____

_____

_____

8. _____

_____

_____

_____

9. _____

_____

_____

_____

10. _____

_____

_____

_____

4

Daily Walk With The Lord

Choose 5 scriptures that are meaningful to you and ones that you use in your daily life to guide you.

1. _____

2. _____

3. _____

4. _____

5. _____

5

Biography

Choose one person from the list below and write a short biography.

You can choose a certain time frame from their life to focus on, an accomplishment in their life they are noted for, or the turning point in their life that made them into who they became.

What do you think may have happened for them to have made the choices they did? Did they pay a price for their choice? Do you think it was worth it to them? Did their trials and tribulations make them stronger?

How did the other people in their life react to their choice? Do you think they may have lost friends over their actions? Gain new friends? Would you describe their choices as worldly or spiritual?

Choose 1 person from the list below or choose a person of your own choice.

1. Fanny Crosby

2. Martin Luther

3. John Wycliffe

4. Joan of Arc

5. Mother Teresa

6. Billy Sunday

7. Dwight Moody

8. J.R.R. Tolkien

9. C. S. Lewis

10. Esther

11. Daniel

12. John Sebastian Bach

13. George Frideric Handel

14. Harriet Beecher Stowe

15. Rembrandt Harmensz Van Rijn

Or you may write of someone of your own choosing who may have influenced or inspired you.

6

Have You Ever Wondered...

I don't believe there is anyone who has read the Bible who hasn't had questions. They may not have anything to do with their faith but just something they may have wondered about. I'm sure you have too. Below are some of these questions and then there is space for you to write questions you yourself have wondered about. Use the space below to write about your thoughts on the questions given.

1. What does God look like?

_____

_____

_____

_____

_____

_____

_____

_____

_____

_____

_____

2. It can be very confusing in Genesis where it says, *'In the beginning there was light,'* and then also say God was always – no beginning or end.

_____

_____

_____

_____

_____

_____

_____

_____

_____

_____

_____

4) What happens when someone dies?

_____

_____

_____

_____

_____

_____

_____

_____

_____

_____

5) Do you sometimes feel, 'I have failed many times and am afraid because of that I won't go to heaven?'

_____

_____

_____

_____

_____

_____

_____

_____

_____

_____

What are some questions you may have wondered about. Write them below.

_____

_____

_____

_____

_____

_____

_____

_____

7

Christian Music

The hymns we sing in church are songs of praise we sing that are not only pleasing to God, but they help us to focus on the Lord, and are meant to edify us. Hymns have been sung since the time of Moses. The songs we sing should come from the heart.

Several hymns we are familiar with were written after an event that inspired the writer to write the hymn.

One example of this is 'It Is Well With My Soul.'

Do a little research and discover what occurred that inspired Horatio Spafford to write this moving hymn.

_____

_____

_____

_____

_____

_____

_____

_____

Read the story of how your favorite hymn or Christian song came about, what inspired the writer to write it.

How does it make you feel when you hear this song or when you sing it yourself? Does it make you feel closer to God?

Name of song or hymn: _____

_____

_____

_____

_____

_____

_____

_____

_____

_____

_____

_____

Perhaps you may be inspired to write your own song about your faith and what it means to you. Try to write your own song. You can use the melody of a song you are familiar with to put the words to. If you prefer, write a poem.

Name of song or poem you wrote:

_____

Story behind the song or poem you wrote:

_____

_____

_____

_____

_____

_____

_____

_____

_____

_____

_____

Lyrics to your song or poem (if you put it to the melody of a song put the name of that below also)

8

My Positive Influence

Who has influenced you in a positive way in your Christian walk?

To influence one is the capacity to have an effect on the character, development, or behavior of someone.

For someone to have a positive influence on you is someone who cares enough to spend the time to encourage or lead you.

Perhaps it is someone you have seen and been inspired by and it is their example that has influenced you and inspired you to strive to be a better person.

Write about the person who has most inspired you and how they have done so.

_____

_____

_____

_____

_____

9

Inspirational Quotes

Old sayings and quotes that impact us in a positive way are meant to inspire us.

Years before I ever thought of becoming a writer I had a creative writing teacher in high school that at the beginning of the class would write a saying or quote on the blackboard. The only instructions given us were to start writing and turn in our papers at the end of the class. At the time I thought that was the laziest teacher I ever had, yet decades later I still use these writing exercises quite frequently. Whether they are used to incorporate into a story or as a means to make us think they can be a very effective tool in not only our writing but to use in our own lives.
...So, start writing.

On the following pages are 10 inspirational quotes or sayings.
Each day take one of these quotes and write how it will influence you, what it means to you, or a story about it.

1. Sweep around your own front door

2. If you don't have something good to say about somebody, don't say anything at all.

---

3. You can be much more influential if people are not aware of your influence.

_____

_____

_____

_____

_____

_____

_____

_____

_____

_____

_____

_____

_____

_____

_____

4. I cried because I had no shoes until I saw a man who had no feet.

_____

_____

_____

_____

_____

_____

_____

_____

_____

_____

_____

_____

_____

_____

_____

_____

5. Let your light shine so bright that others can see their way out of the dark.

_____

_____

_____

_____

_____

_____

_____

_____

_____

_____

_____

_____

_____

_____

_____

6. Be the person you want to see in others.

_____

_____

_____

_____

_____

_____

_____

_____

_____

_____

_____

_____

_____

_____

_____

7. Best friends aren't the ones who make you feel the best, they're the ones who bring out the best in you.

8. Time is free, but it's priceless. You can't own it, but you can use it. You can't keep it, but you can spend it. Once you're lost it, you can never get it back.

_____

_____

_____

_____

_____

_____

_____

_____

_____

_____

_____

_____

_____

_____

_____

_____

9. We don't lose friends, we learn who our real ones are.

_____

_____

_____

_____

_____

_____

_____

_____

_____

_____

_____

_____

_____

_____

10. Deal with the faults of others as gently as you do your own.

10

Looking Within

*Answer one question a day for a month.
You can keep your answers short, but give them some
thought before you answer.*

1. Who is your hero?

_____

_____

_____

_____

_____

_____

_____

_____

_____

_____

2. How do people describe you? How would you describe yourself?

_____

_____

_____

_____

_____

_____

_____

_____

3. What type person is your best friend? Do they have good quality traits you would like to emulate? What is it about them that drew you to them as a good friend?

_____

_____

_____

_____

_____

_____

_____

_____

_____

_____

4. What is more important to you at this time: your everlasting soul or your looks?

_____

_____

_____

_____

_____

_____

_____

_____

_____

5. What is more important to you: Being popular or standing up for what is right?

_____

_____

_____

_____

_____

_____

_____

6. What bad habits do you have that you would like to overcome?

_____

_____

_____

_____

_____

_____

_____

_____

_____

_____

7. What are you most proud of concerning yourself?

_____

_____

_____

_____

_____

_____

_____

_____

8. How do you handle it when someone makes a catty, snide remark about you; whether it's about something you're wearing, your hair, something you said, or an opinion you have about a certain matter?

_____

_____

_____

_____

_____

_____

_____

_____

9. Peer pressure can be really tough. When someone trys to talk you into doing something you know is wrong, figure out a plan of how to deflect it so the next time it comes up you have a plan on how to handle it.

_____

_____

_____

_____

_____

_____

_____

_____

_____

_____

10. You are unique, you are special, you are loved by God...what do *you think is special about you?*

_____

_____

_____

_____

_____

_____

_____

_____

11. Do you struggle with anger issues? If you struggle with controlling your temper, come up with a plan ahead of time for when you next become angry on how you will respond – *and stick to it.*

_____

_____

_____

_____

_____

_____

_____

_____

_____

12. How do you cope with stress? Do you worry about things needlessly? What can you do to overcome this?

_____

_____

_____

_____

_____

_____

_____

_____

13. Are you a glass half full or half empty type person?

_____

_____

_____

_____

_____

_____

_____

_____

14. Do you speak up for what you believe in or think to yourself that you don't want to be ridiculed for your beliefs or for "being different from the crowd"?

_____

_____

_____

_____

_____

_____

_____

_____

_____

_____

15. How is your endurance: Do you stick with something to the end?

_____

_____

_____

_____

_____

_____

_____

_____

16. Is it easy for you to forgive? Is it easy for you to admit when you are wrong and to ask for forgiveness?

_____

_____

_____

_____

_____

_____

_____

_____

17. Are you a leader or a follower?

_____

_____

_____

_____

_____

_____

_____

_____

_____

18. Are you a person who easily gets along with others or are you contentious?

_____

_____

_____

_____

_____

_____

_____

_____

19. Do you show your parents, grandparents, neighbors, teachers, and others the respect you should?

_____

_____

_____

_____

_____

_____

_____

_____

_____

_____

20. Is there a relationship you could do better at? Perhaps with a parent, sibling, or someone who feels left out at school?

_____

_____

_____

_____

_____

_____

_____

_____

21. Are you dependable?

_____

_____

_____

_____

_____

_____

_____

_____

22. What are you afraid of?

_____

_____

_____

_____

_____

_____

_____

_____

_____

23. Is there something you don't do because you are afraid of failure?

_____

_____

_____

_____

_____

_____

_____

_____

24. When you are in a social environment, do you bury your face in your phone instead of interacting with the people you are with? How do you feel when others do this and ignore you? Do you find this to be rude?

_____

_____

_____

_____

_____

_____

_____

_____

25. What do others most like about you?

_____

_____

_____

_____

_____

_____

_____

_____

_____

_____

26. What goals do you have for when you finish high school and after?

_____

_____

_____

_____

_____

_____

_____

_____

27. Are you a procrastinator? If so, what should you do in the future to overcome this?

_____

_____

_____

_____

_____

_____

_____

_____

_____

28. What do you like to do in your spare time?

_____

_____

_____

_____

_____

_____

_____

_____

_____

29. Cyberbullying can be extremely hurtful and damaging to others. People feel freer with hurtful words when they aren't face to face with that person. If you are on the receiving end of this it can cause a loss of reputation, lies being spread about you, depression, and even suicide. Make a promise to yourself that you won't take part in being a cyberbully and do what you can to put an end to it on the part of your friends. Taking a positive stance on this issue, what are your plans to take on this issue head on?

_____

_____

_____

_____

_____

_____

_____

_____

30. How much time do you spend on social media? Is this productive, hurtful, a waste of your time? How can you turn your social media time into something positive?

_____

_____

_____

_____

_____

_____

_____

_____

_____

Are there any notes you would like to add to your thoughts on the questions above or anything that hasn't been addressed

_____

_____

_____

_____

_____

11

Journal

Throughout history people were inclined to keep journals. Their journals could have been their daily thoughts, trials , tribulations and triumphs, or it could have been notes on their business life or what was happening in the world at the time.

Start keeping your own daily journal.

Below is a starting point for you to start your journal.

Date: _____

_____

_____

_____

_____

_____

_____

_____

Date: _____

Date: _____

Date: _____

Date: _____

Date: _____

_____

_____

_____

_____

_____

_____

_____

_____

_____

_____

Date: _____

_____

_____

_____

_____

_____

Date: _____

Date: _____

Date: _____

12

Selfless Acts

It pleases the Lord when we do a kind act for others.

Throughout the next few weeks or months pick one of these selfless acts once a day, once a week, or when you feel so inclined to do something nice for someone and write about your experience, how it affected the other person, and how it made you feel.

While you will find that you have made someone else's day a better day; you will also find that you feel uplifted, too.

1. Set the table or help make dinner for your mom.

_____

_____

_____

_____

_____

_____

_____

_____

_____

_____

2. Reach out to others in a positive way on social media. Be an inspiration and invite three of your friends to do the same. Have each of them encourage three more people to do the same and pass it on. See how quickly the idea grows.

_____

_____

_____

_____

_____

_____

_____

_____

_____

_____

3. Get out and watch the sun rise or set, look up at the stars at night. Look at the beautiful flowers and the birds flying and singing their songs. What else do you see of God's creation in nature that you are thankful for? Thank God for his creation and His many blessings.

_____

_____

_____

_____

_____

_____

_____

_____

_____

4. Have a '*No Negativity Day*' – a day of no complaints, but only praise and thankfulness.

_____

_____

_____

5. Collect food to give to a needy family

6. Encourage someone by a kind word or compliment.

_____

_____

_____

_____

_____

_____

_____

_____

7. Perhaps there is a new mother in your church or neighborhood. With a new baby one thing new mothers discover is a lack of time. Offer to rock or feed the baby while she rests or gets some housework done or offer to wash and fold the clothes, play with the other children, or something you know she needs done.

_____

_____

_____

_____

_____

_____

_____

_____

_____

_____

8. Let your dad know how much you appreciate all he does for you.

_____

_____

_____

_____

_____

_____

_____

_____

_____

9. Give someone flowers or a small gift, it can be a homemade gift – not for a special occasion, but just because...

_____

_____

_____

_____

_____

_____

_____

_____

10. If you have a social media page put out a scripture a day or week for encouragement to those who read it

_____

_____

_____

_____

_____

_____

_____

_____

_____

_____

11. Do something nice for your siblings.

_____

_____

_____

_____

_____

_____

_____

_____

12. Tell someone special in your life how much they mean to you.

_____

_____

_____

_____

_____

_____

_____

_____

13. Volunteer: It could be at a food bank, you could collect socks or blankets for the homeless, fill shoeboxes with small goodies for Christmas, mow the lawn for an elderly shut in, visit shut ins, volunteer at a children's hospital, help your mother clean house, or something that you come up with on your own...

_____

_____

_____

_____

_____

_____

_____

_____

_____

14. Pick up the phone and call your grandparents and let them know how important they are to you – they will be overwhelmed with joy.

_____

_____

_____

_____

_____

_____

_____

_____

_____

15. Look around you at God's creation and focus on one thing. When you pray let Him know how thankful you are for His magnificent creation.

_____

_____

_____

_____

_____

_____

_____

_____

16. Do a kind act for someone who has wronged you in the past, even if that kind act is forgiving them.

_____

_____

_____

_____

_____

_____

_____

17. Do a 5K run for a charity and encourage others to join you.

_____

_____

_____

_____

_____

_____

_____

_____

_____

18. Tell someone how they changed your life for the better, how they are an inspiration to you.

_____

_____

_____

_____

_____

_____

_____

_____

_____

19. Are you *really* busy or filling time? Are you using your time wisely? Use your time to do something for someone else.

_____

_____

_____

_____

_____

_____

_____

_____

_____

20. Smile at your mom for no reason other than to let her know you care and love her.

_____

_____

_____

_____

_____

_____

_____

_____

_____

21. Be happy for someone else's victory or opportunity...and let them know you are truly happy for them (and mean it!)

_____

_____

_____

_____

_____

_____

_____

_____

22. Visit a home for the elderly and ask to visit someone who receives few or no visitors.

_____

_____

_____

_____

_____

_____

_____

_____

23. Don't let someone else's moods bring you down, instead lift them up.

_____

_____

_____

_____

_____

_____

_____

_____

_____

_____

24. If you have done something to hurt someone ask for their forgiveness.

_____

_____

_____

_____

_____

_____

_____

_____

25. If you have your driver's license take a grandparent out for a ice cream sundae; if you don't drive, take over the ingredients and make it at their house and spend some fun time with them.

_____

13

For Your Spiritual Growth

1. Read one scripture everyday at the beginning of the day and keep that in mind throughout the day.

_____

_____

_____

_____

_____

_____

2. Take time everyday to pray.

_____

_____

_____

_____

_____

_____

3. What is God's gift to you? How can you use this gift to give to Him in return?

_____

_____

_____

_____

_____

4. Give thanks for a blessing you have received.

_____

_____

_____

_____

_____

5. Make goals: short and long term (they aren't written in stone, they can be adjusted, but be realistic).

_____

_____

_____

_____

_____

_____

6. In what instance did you not go along with the crowd? How did your friends react? How did it make you feel? Were you grateful for the choice you made later?

_____

_____

_____

_____

_____

7. Spend some time outdoors and listen to the birds sing, watch the wind in the trees while the squirrels scurry about...make notes on what you see, hear, smell, feel...

_____

_____

_____

_____

8. Learn to enjoy quiet time.

_____

_____

_____

_____

_____

9. Read a book that will inspire you then pass it on to someone else.

_____

_____

_____

_____

_____

10. We grow in strength and character when we face difficulties; handle them accordingly; these too shall pass. Contemplate on an instance where you had a rough time with something or someone and how you handled it. Did you make the right choices? How did your reaction make you feel, both at the time and later? Would you handle the situation differently today? How so?

14

Debate

As a Christian you will face many instances when you are questioned as to why you believe in something.

Be prepared. Know the answers and how to respond to these situations.

If your school offers a debate class this is a great opportunity to learn how to debate a topic from both sides without arguing, but with giving opposing viewpoints on a topic.

Choose one of the topics below. You can ask a parent or another student to debate the topic with you having them take the opposing viewpoint.

1. Creation vs. evolution

2. Women's role in the church: should they be allowed to preach or be elders or to take a leadership role

3. The Bible: God given vs. man written

4. Is same sex marriage or relationships acceptable to God

5. Capital punishment

6. Abortion

7. Should stem cell research be allowed?

8. Should schools be teaching secular viewpoints on topics that go against everything Christians believe in?

9. Should prayer be allowed in school?

10. Is baptism required: if so full immersion or sprinkled?

I HOPE YOU ENJOYED THIS BOOK.
IF SO, PLEASE DO TAKE A FEW MINUTES TO
LEAVE FEEDBACK AT AMAZON. I WOULD
APPRECIATE IT VERY MUCH.

BOOK 2 OF THE SERIES, **A HUMBLE SPIRIT'** -
CREATIVE WRITING FOR CHRISTIAN TEENS
IS ALSO AVAILABLE.

THANK YOU AND FEEL FREE TO CONTACT
ME WITH ANY COMMENTS YOU MAY WISH
TO SHARE

ARLINGTONAMELIAPUB@CFL.RR.COM

GOD BLESS,
CHERYL PRYOR

www.ingramcontent.com/pod-product-compliance
Lightning Source LLC
Chambersburg PA
CBHW061957040426
42447CB00010B/1787